NEW YORK

UNION SQUARE KIDS and the distinctive Union Square Kids logo are trademarks of Hachette Book Group, Inc.

ISBN 978-1-4549-6167-3

Library of Congress Control Number 2025024866

Union Square Kids books may be purchased in bulk for business, educational, or promotional use. For more information, please contact your local bookseller or the Hachette Book Group's Special Markets department at special.markets@hbgusa.com.

Printed in Guangdong, China

Lot #:

2 4 6 8 10 9 7 5 3 1

08/25

unionsquareandco.com

Text by Emma Roberts
Book design by Ashtyn Botterill
Edited by Helen Brown

For Livia Rose. May you grow to know the fierce power of using your voice.—E.R.

For Tina. For planting seeds of bold curiosity, compassion and love as action.—S.H.

5 Minute Genius Stories

The Women Who Won the Vote

Written by Emma Roberts
Illustrated by Seobhan Hope

How to use this book

In this book you'll find **ten genius stories** to read, each one just **5 minutes long**.

At the end of each story, explore an informative **"all about"** spread.

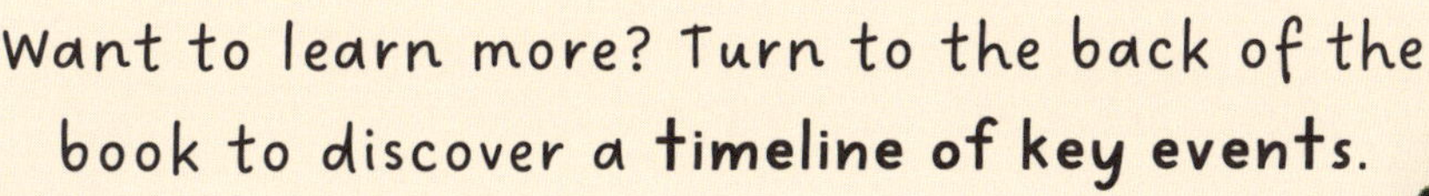

Want to learn more? Turn to the back of the book to discover a **timeline of key events**.

NEW YORK

WHO WERE THE WOMEN WHO WON THE VOTE?

Women and girls of different ages, races, backgrounds, and communities fought for the right to vote. While this selection highlights ten of the brave women who spoke up for women's suffrage in the United States and the United Kingdom, they are just a handful among countless others whose courage shaped history.

SOJOURNER TRUTH

c.1797–1883

A formerly enslaved woman who gave one of the most famous speeches in the history of women's rights.

Page 8

SUSAN B. ANTHONY

1820-1906

One of America's most well-known women's right activists. She was arrested and put in jail for the cause.

Page 18

LUCY STONE

1818-1893

A brave voice for women's rights, she was the first white American woman to keep her birth surname after marriage.

Page 28

EMMELINE PANKHURST

1858-1928

A fierce English suffragette who brought the motto "Deeds Not Words" and her methods of protest to the US.

Page 38

ALICE PAUL

1885-1977

A determined leader who wasn't afraid to cause trouble in the fight for women's suffrage.

Page 48

IDA B. WELLS

1862-1931

A journalist and educator, she worked tirelessly for African American women's voices to be heard.

Page 58

BESSIE WATSON

1900-1992

A Scottish child suffragette who played bagpipes to support imprisoned women protesters.

Page 68

ROSALIE JONES

1883-1978

A fearless campaigner who led women on protest hikes to attract the attention of the press to the cause.

Page 78

THE SILENT SENTINELS

1917-1918

A group of women who stood in silent protest for months on end outside the White House.

Page 88

MARIE LOUISE BOTTINEAU BALDWIN

1863-1952

A Turtle Mountain Ojibwe (Chippewa) Nation lawyer who highlighted her ancestors' support for women's suffrage.

Page 98

WHICH 5-MINUTE GENIUS STORY WILL YOU READ TODAY?

SOJOURNER TRUTH

Delivering Her Legendary Speech on Inequality

On a warm Ohio morning in May 1851, a packed Women's Rights Convention was getting started in Akron's Old Stone Church. The topic for discussion?

The unfair differences between what women and men were allowed to do. One of these differences was suffrage—the right to vote, which wasn't allowed for women.

As the morning went on, a woman asked to say a few words. The platform was given to her, and the woman known as **Sojourner Truth** began to speak.
WOMEN'S RIGHTS CONVENTION

Sojourner was named Isabella at birth, on the farm in upstate New York where she and her family were enslaved.

When she became a free woman later in life, she bravely took one of the families who enslaved her to court for their terrible wrongdoing. She won.

She chose the name 'Sojourner Truth' for herself in 1843, with her first name reflecting her new life as a traveling preacher.

Sojourner had a powerful voice that made people stop and listen to what she had to say. She was also almost six feet tall, and that drew people's attention, too.

She stood before the audience of mainly white, rich, educated women and delivered a rousing speech that began, "I am a woman's rights."

Her words were cleverly chosen, challenging racism as well as sexism.

Sojourner gave examples of the back-breaking physical work she'd had to do while enslaved.

So, she pointed out, because she had done work that was thought of as "men's work," shouldn't she enjoy the same rights as men?

And in the same way, shouldn't Black people like her have the same rights as white people?

Sojourner Truth's speech was written down by a friend present at the conference, a newspaper editor called Marius Robinson.

Sojourner herself had never had the opportunity to learn to read or write, but Marius published his account of her words in *The Anti-Slavery Bugle* soon after.

But her Akron, Ohio speech would go on to be considered one of the most important in the history of the women's rights movement.

What is SUFFRAGE?

"Suffrage" means the right to vote in elections, like voting for the president in the United States or for members of parliament in the United Kingdom.

At the point of Sojourner Truth's speech, the only people who could vote in America were **white men**, and in some states only white men could **own property**.

Women's suffrage is the right of women to vote.

In the early days, the fight for women's rights wasn't just about voting, it was also for women to have **access to education**, or for wives and husbands to have **equal rights in owning property**.

Abolitionists—people who campaigned for an end to slavery—and **suffragists** often shared the same aim of freeing people from the injustices placed upon them.

Women who became leaders in the movement for suffrage learned about successful campaigning from the **anti-slavery movement**. They often used the same tactics in their fight for women's rights.

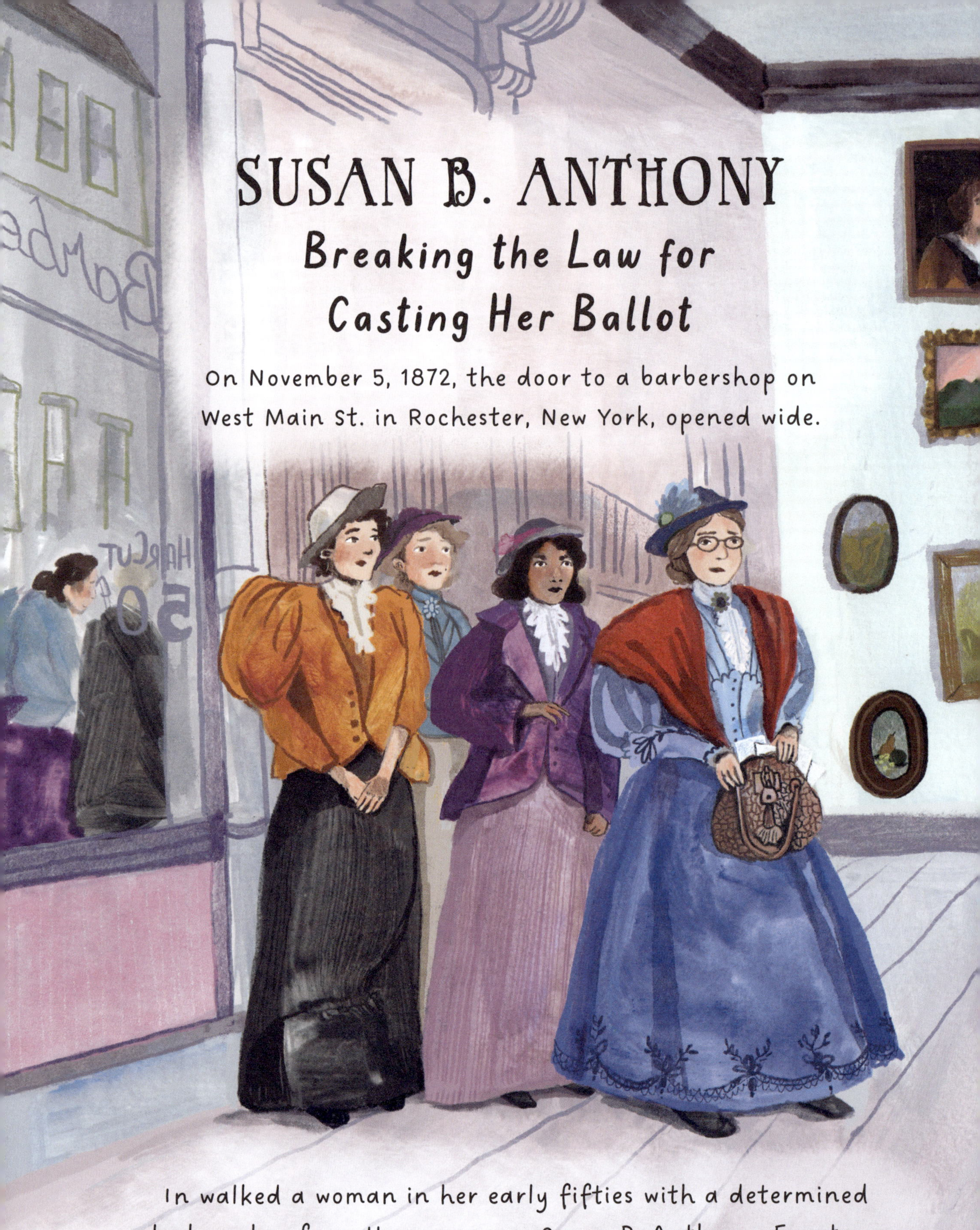

SUSAN B. ANTHONY

Breaking the Law for Casting Her Ballot

On November 5, 1872, the door to a barbershop on West Main St. in Rochester, New York, opened wide.

In walked a woman in her early fifties with a determined look on her face. Her name was Susan B. Anthony. Fourteen other women followed her inside, including her three sisters.

They were all there to do something that they knew could land them in jail. They were going to cast a vote in the presidential election.

These fifteen campaigners wanted to vote, but they also wanted to test out a new argument for women's suffrage called the New Departure. They argued the Constitution of the United States already guaranteed a woman's right to vote.

Susan and her fellow suffragists were expecting to be stopped by officials, and planned to take anyone who stood in their way to court.

As Susan approached the poll worker and asked for a ballot, she was shocked to be handed one without challenge.

But she was also reminded of the unexpected thing that had happened just a few days earlier when she had gone to register to vote.

Then, the election officials had challenged her, but she had debated the New Departure with them for an hour and, to her surprise, they had allowed her to register.

Within minutes, Susan had cast her vote and left the polling place.

It was an act of defiance that saw her arrested two weeks later, and put on trial seven months after that.

Her voting made national news, as did the coverage of her court case, in which she had hoped to be sentenced so she could appeal all the way to the Supreme Court.

But the judge wasn't going to let Susan and her argument reach the highest court in the land and gain more public attention along the way. He fined her $100 and closed the case.

Although Susan didn't get the chance to argue the New Departure strategy in court, she had proved the notion of many anti-suffrage campaigners wrong . . .

Society hadn't collapsed when a woman voted!

The "NEW DEPARTURE"

In 1871, the organization Susan B. Anthony led, the National Woman Suffrage Association, decided to follow a new plan for winning the vote. It was called the New Departure.

The New Departure **used the 14th Amendment of the Constitution of the United States.**

The 14th Amendment promised citizenship rights to **all persons born in the United States.**

Susan B. Anthony believed that **voting was one of the citizenship rights** mentioned in the amendment, and she wanted to prove the word "persons" meant women as well as men.

So Susan and her fellow suffragists tested their argument by trying to **register and then vote.**

But in 1875, the **Supreme Court** decreed that voting was not a citizenship right, and the women were forced to abandon the New Departure.

LUCY STONE

Keeping Her Name After Getting Married

On the Stone family farm in West Brockfield, Massachusetts, a bride smiled as she smoothed down the special lace she'd added to the collar of her favorite dress.

It was 1855, and there was a hum of anticipation in the May-Day air.

Today was the wedding of the women's rights campaigner Lucy Stone to Henry Blackwell, a businessman. The couple first met in Cincinnati, where Lucy was giving a lecture.

Friends and relations were gathered at the farm, looking forward to a day to remember.

But it would be a memorable day for more reasons than one. Newspapers from South Carolina to Massachusetts had been buzzing with opinion about this wedding for a while.

The happy couple's special day represented something radical and scandalous—because they wanted theirs to be a marriage of equality.

At a time when a woman could not keep her own wages,

or own her own home,

or exist at all in the eyes of the law once she became a wife, Lucy believed that marriage was not fair for women.

Henry agreed, and so, they had prepared a statement together which explained how their marriage would be protecting Lucy's equal rights. They read it aloud and published it on the day of the wedding.

But Lucy also took a huge step further in her protest at the inequality between men and women in marriage.

She kept her birth surname, Stone, rather than taking Henry's name and becoming Mrs. Blackwell. In Lucy's words, "My name is the symbol of my identity and must not be lost."

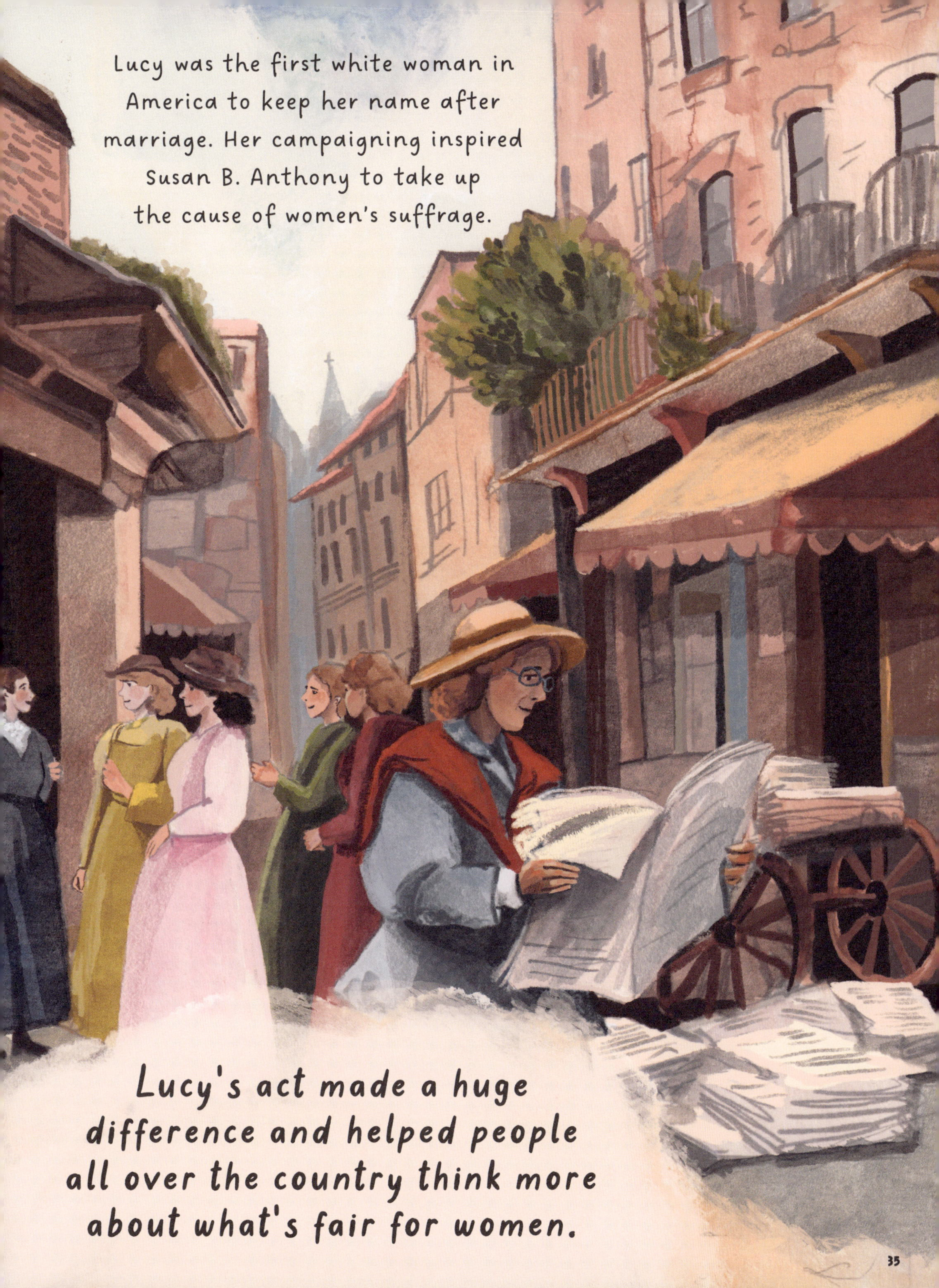

Lucy was the first white woman in America to keep her name after marriage. Her campaigning inspired Susan B. Anthony to take up the cause of women's suffrage.

Lucy's act made a huge difference and helped people all over the country think more about what's fair for women.

THE WOMEN'S RIGHTS CONVENTION
That Brought People from Far and Wide

The very first national women's rights convention was held in Worcester, Massachusetts in October 1850. Lucy Stone was one of the organizers.

The event had more than **1,000 attendees**, both men and women, who came from eleven different states.

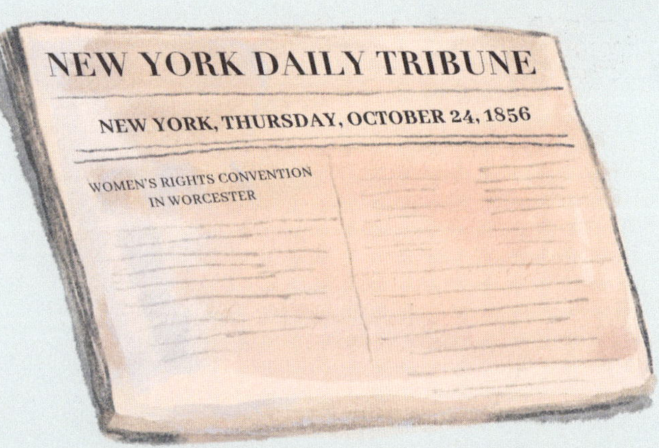

NEW YORK DAILY TRIBUNE

NEW YORK, THURSDAY, OCTOBER 24, 1856

WOMEN'S RIGHTS CONVENTION IN WORCESTER

According to the *New-York Daily Tribune*: "if a larger place could have been had, many more thousands would have attended."

Sojourner Truth was one of the speakers, and addressed the need to fight for the rights of enslaved women.

Lucy spoke on a **woman's right to vote.**

Other women talked about being able to **study** and work in professions like medicine.

Lucy published copies of the **Proceedings** from the convention a year later, in 1851, to **raise money for the cause.**

The conference was criticized by some newspapers and magazines. But this only drew more attention to the message the women wanted to share with the public.

EMMELINE PANKHURST

Bringing the Fight to America

On November 13, 1913, an excited crowd waited expectantly in Parsons Theater, Hartford, Connecticut. The English woman who'd just mounted the stage before them was standing in front of a banner in the British suffragette colors of purple, white, and green.

She was Emmeline Pankhurst, suffragette and leader of the Women's Social and Political Union (WSPU) in the United Kingdom.

The women in the WSPU were tired of waiting and talking politely about getting the vote, only to be ignored by politicians. So they decided they had to act, choosing the motto "Deeds Not Words."

Emmeline was here to spread the word to a curious American audience.

Emmeline surveyed the eager faces in front of her, clasped her hands behind her back, and began.

"I am here as a soldier who has temporarily left the field of battle in order to explain . . . what civil war is like when civil war is waged by women," she said, before telling the audience she had been to prison many times for protesting.

It wasn't irresponsible to protest by doing things like breaking windows, she explained.

Violent protest was the only option available to women to bring about change, because they did not have the option to vote for change.

After all, Emmeline argued, American men had protested by throwing precious cargoes of tea into Boston harbor in 1773 when the British government refused to listen to them!

But, unlike male protestors, she said, the women in the WSPU didn't believe in hurting people. They were going through all of their struggles—

all of the time spent in freezing prison cells,

the violent treatment at the hands of police and prison guards,

the hunger strikes—so they could bring about a better world for everyone.

With the vote, women would be able to fight for a better life for themselves, but also their communities.

Emmeline Pankhurst left America after her 1913 tour having raised significant money for the WSPU's work (almost $700,000 today.)

She also left behind an inspired group of American women determined to fight in a similar way for their suffrage.

The difference between SUFFRAGIST and SUFFRAGETTE

"Suffragist" was the name for a supporter of suffrage who used non-violent methods like talking to politicians to try and win the vote for women.

The British women using violent methods were known as **"suffragettes."** This word, intended to be a patronizing version of "suffragist," was made up by a British newspaper in order to make fun of the women of the WSPU.

"Suffragettes" was first used in the Daily Mail in 1906

Instead, Emmeline and the other women proudly adopted the word as their own, even publishing a newspaper called *The Suffragette*.

The suffragettes were regularly put in **prison** for their actions, and often given harsh sentences.

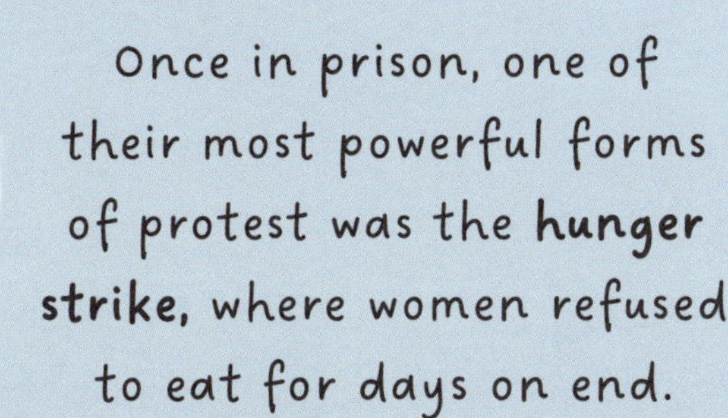

Once in prison, one of their most powerful forms of protest was the **hunger strike,** where women refused to eat for days on end.

Prisons couldn't risk public outcry over a suffragette dying on hunger strike, so they **force-fed** them. A rubber tube was inserted through the nose into the stomach to deliver liquid food. Emmeline's daughters, Christabel and Sylvia, endured this ordeal.

ALICE PAUL

Disrupting the Mayor's Banquet to Make Her Voice Heard

On November 9, 1909, twenty-four-year-old Alice Paul dropped to a crouch in a dark corner of the gallery of the grand Guildhall building in London, England. A young nurse, Amelia Brown, huddled beside her.

Both women held their breath as a policeman walked by so closely his cape brushed against Alice's hair. He didn't notice them.

When the coast was clear, Alice nudged Amelia and the pair uncurled from their uncomfortable position. Alice breathed out, feeling resistance from the ties of her scrubwoman's apron fastened tightly around her middle.

But these were no scrubwomen. They were suffragettes in disguise, and they were on a secret mission!

Alice, a young American student in England, had first come to the United Kingdom to study economics at the University of Birmingham.

It was there she had attended a talk by Christabel Pankhurst, and had come out full of enthusiasm for the suffragettes' methods of protest.

Now, a year or so later, she was studying in London as well as fighting, suffragette style, for the vote.

Alice and Amelia had been inside the grand Guildhall building since 9 a.m. that morning. The Lord Mayor was hosting a banquet in the evening, and they had dressed as cleaners to enter with the rest of the staff.
They had been trying to go unnoticed all day and were now hiding in the gallery of the banquet hall.

Several hours later, British Prime Minister H. H. Asquith got to his feet to deliver a speech to the distinguished roomful of guests in the hall below.

Alice knew it was time to do what they'd come for . . .

When the prime minister paused for breath, Alice summoned all her strength and yelled at the top of her voice, "How about votes for women?"

It was as if Alice had thrown a bomb, not words.

Chaos broke out as many police officers on duty searched for the wily suffragettes, hauling Alice and Amelia off to jail when they were discovered.

In Holloway prison, Alice went on hunger strike and suffered force feeding twice a day for most of her thirty-day sentence.

After recovering from her ordeal she returned home to America, bringing the British suffragette tactics back with her.

Making Women's SUFFRAGE a National Matter

When Alice returned to the US, she set to work, pushing the cause of women's suffrage forward with her determined activism.

As part of the leadership of the **National American Woman Suffrage Association** (NAWSA) Alice organized a huge suffrage parade in Washington D.C. for March 3, 1913.

She cleverly chose the day before President Woodrow Wilson's **inauguration** because she knew Washington D.C. would already be full of people who'd come there to celebrate their new president.

But Alice's approach to winning the vote was more extreme than that of the NAWSA, and Alice broke away. She eventually set up her own political party in 1916, the **National Women's Party** (NWP) with Lucy Burns, an American suffragette whom Alice had first met in British prison.

By 1916, some women were able to vote in some US states, like **California and Kansas.**

However, the NWP's goal was an amendment to the Constitution so **women's suffrage would become protected by a national law.** Unfortunately, President Woodrow Wilson did not have the same goal.

IDA B. WELLS

Marching Together or Not At All

A smartly dressed woman wearing a white sash stood on Pennsylvania Avenue in Washington, D.C. on March 3, 1913, as the first national women's suffrage protest parade marched past.

The woman was Ida B. Wells of Chicago, Illinois, and she had come to Washington, D.C. to take part in the parade and protest for votes for women.

But organizer Alice Paul had said Ida would have to march at the back because she was African American.

There was no way Ida was going to agree to this racist rule.

She knew the organizers were trying to segregate the march to appeal to women and men from the Southern states, where segregation was enforced.

Ida would march where she wanted to march, and where she belonged—with the other suffragists from Illinois.

Otherwise, she would not march at all.

She scanned the parade. Some protestors held banners, others locked arms against the hostile crowd. African American women stood out, representing hometowns; colleges; careers, like medicine; and passions, like music.

Then her eyes landed on a familiar and welcome face—her friend Mary Church Terrell, one of the first African American women to go to college in the United States. Mary wasn't marching at the back.

She was in the midst of the parade, carrying a flag with the motto of the National Association of Colored Women's Clubs, which she and Ida both helped to start: "Lifting as We Climb".

Eventually, Ida found what she had been searching for—ever since lawyer Inez Milholland had trotted past on her magnificent white horse at the start of the parade.

Her friends from the Illinois delegation, Belle Squire and Virginia Brooks!

It was time to go.

She slipped out of the crowd and calmly wove her way into the group of Illinois women, her footsteps falling into time with theirs.

Ida marched on.

Black Women's SUFFRAGE

Ida B. Wells once wrote: "Our women should be as firm in standing up for their principles as the Southern women are for their prejudices."

During the early 1900s, African American women were fighting for the right to vote while also fighting against the other injustices placed upon them because of **people's racist attitudes**.

Ida founded the **Alpha Suffrage Club** in Chicago in January 1913, alongside her white allies Belle Squire and Virginia Brooks. Its purpose was to educate and empower African American women.

The Alpha Suffrage Club taught on civic matters, including why it was so important for African American women to **vote**.

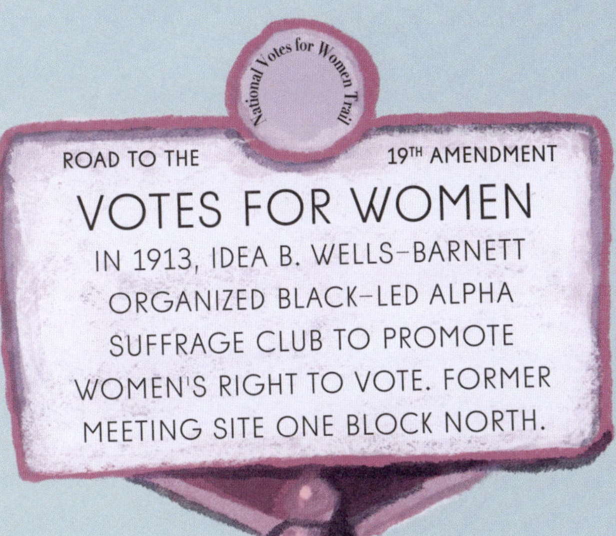

It also published a **newsletter** to share the work of the club with a bigger audience.

The Alpha Suffrage Record

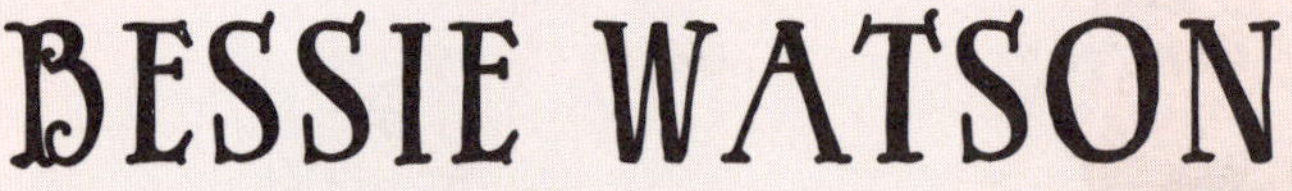

BESSIE WATSON

Playing Bagpipes for the Suffragette Cause

On a chilly autumn day in 1900s Scotland, Bessie Watson moistened her lips and drew a breath of air into her lungs.

She took a nervous glance up at the cold stone walls of Edinburgh's Calton Jail, then drew her narrow shoulders back in defiance.

Bessie wasn't yet a teenager, but she was a committed supporter of women's suffrage and had important work to do.

Inside Calton's cells, the suffragettes imprisoned there pricked up their ears. Young Bessie Watson was back to pipe for them!
The familiar music made their hearts swell with hope.

These suffragettes were being kept in unpleasant conditions and were often subject to harsh treatment—all for fighting for their right to vote.

For the women locked up in Calton Jail, their spirits were lifted . . .

knowing that Bessie was out there playing her bagpipes just for them.

As Bessie played, the image of one of her most treasured memories popped into her head.

Bessie had played her pipes at an earlier suffragette march, and had been gifted a brooch as a thank you.

The brooch was given to her by Christabel Pankhurst.

It was in the shape of the mighty Queen Boadicea in her chariot, and young Bessie thought of Ms. Pankhurst as being just as mighty. Bessie was proud to be a suffragette, just like Ms. Pankhurst.

After a spirited thirty minutes, Bessie finished playing and packed her pipes, already thinking about her next visit to Calton Jail.

The young piper would return, as she wanted the brave suffragettes to know they weren't alone in their fight.

Sometimes, Bessie was called on late at night to pipe for suffragettes released from prison,

or when they were leaving for their journey to other jails.

And, now and again, she was even allowed to leave school early to play!

Bessie was small, but her contribution to the suffragette cause was mighty.

Suffragette SYMBOLS

Suffragettes wore and carried items to publicly show their support for a woman's right to vote.

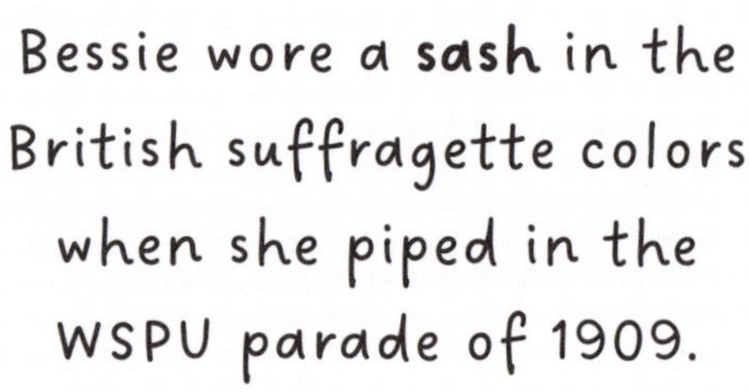

Bessie wore a **sash** in the British suffragette colors when she piped in the WSPU parade of 1909.

Purple for dignity

Green for hope

White for respectability

VOTES FOR WOMEN

Colorful banners with slogans and messages were also displayed at parades.

The earliest American color of women's suffrage was a **golden yellow.** Later, Alice Paul's National Woman's Party combined it with the British colors of purple and white.

Just as soldiers are awarded medals for bravery, **the Queen Boadicea brooch** was issued to suffragettes for their own acts of valor.

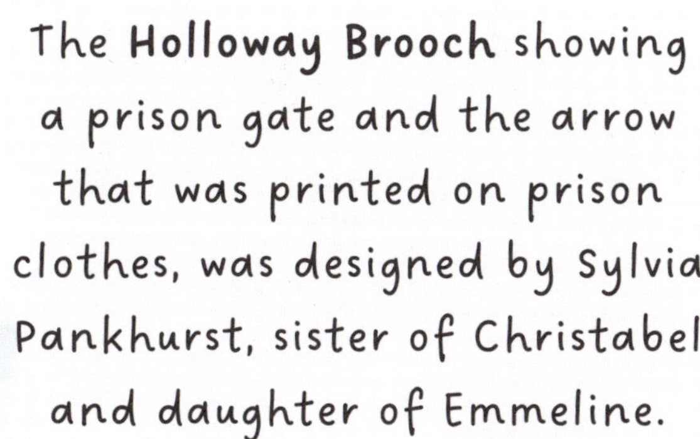

The **Holloway Brooch** showing a prison gate and the arrow that was printed on prison clothes, was designed by Sylvia Pankhurst, sister of Christabel and daughter of Emmeline.

The **Jailed for Freedom** brooch was given to US suffragettes who had gone to prison for the cause.

"GENERAL" ROSALIE JONES

Gathering Her "Troops" to Hike for Suffrage

Rosalie Jones pulled her long cloak tight to protect against the January chill. It was the first day of 1914, and the first day of a new protest.

She adjusted her bag, emblazoned with the words "The Woman Voter," and smiled as she enjoyed the warm presence of the women at her side.

Rosalie called herself "the General" because she was about to lead her "troops" in a grueling 166 mile hike from the Bronx, New York, to the state capitol in Albany.

She also knew the name would cause a stir and gain attention from the press.

This wasn't the first time General Jones had hiked to raise awareness of women's suffrage.

Her first hike for suffrage was on this same route, two years earlier, in December 1912. It was the first of its kind and was reported on in lots of newspapers.

The same media stir happened with her 250-mile hike to Washington, D.C. for the great parade of 1913.

But it was now New Year's Day 1914 and women still didn't have the right to vote. So they were back on the road to demonstrate their commitment.

Six days later, after walking more than 160 miles, on roads in terrible condition and suffering abuse from anti-suffrage protestors,

three of the eleven original hikers approached the outskirts of Albany: General Jones, "Colonel" Ida Craft, and "Corporal" Martha Klatchken.

The exhausted women felt a sudden burst of energy enlivening their weary bodies as they heard the sound of cheering up ahead.

Then the sound of drums and fife flutes!

A noisy crowd, two hundred strong, escorted the brave women on their final miles to the Capitol, where the general, colonel, and corporal met with politicians and pressed "Votes for Women" buttons into their hands.

Rosalie wasn't excited to go on yet another enormous hike, but she vowed: "We shall march next year . . . and every year thereafter until women are granted suffrage."

Rosalie knew that her and her troops' efforts made a great story for the newspapers, and that would only lead to more attention for their cause.

Getting Attention from the PRESS

"Our weapon is public opinion" was a campaign slogan of the women's suffrage movement in the early 20th century.

They knew that getting **writers and photographers to report on their protests** was an effective way to spread their message to the public.

The now famous **photograph of Emmeline Pankhurst** being arrested outside Buckingham Palace was printed widely.

It was included on the front page of The Daily Mirror in the United Kingdom

And also in The Baltimore News.

General Rosalie Jones knew how to get the attention of the press, with her hikes making **great headlines** in newspapers.

25 SUFFRAGETTES START HIKE FROM NEW YORK TO ALBANY TO PUSH 'CAUSE'

Rosalie even went up in an airplane to scatter **suffrage leaflets** from the air—and she made sure that reporters wrote about it, too!

THE SILENT SENTINELS

Peacefully Protesting at the White House

"We may not be admitted within the doors, but we can at least stand at the gates. We may not be allowed to raise our voices and speak to the President, but we can address him just the same, because our message to him will be inscribed upon the banners which we will carry in our hands. Let us post our silent sentinels at the gates of the White House."

The rousing words of Harriot Stanton Blatch, a prominent figure in the women's suffrage movement, echoed in the minds of a group of National Woman's Party (NWP) suffragettes standing by the White House gates.

As President Wilson passed by on his way inside, the women straightened their backs and tightened their grips on the banners they were holding.

They were silent, but their message to their President was loud and clear.

Since January 10, 1917, suffragettes such as Alice Paul, Mary Church Terrell, and Lucy Burns had stood in silent protest daily—except Sundays—by the White House's black railings.

It was now November 1917, and the Silent Sentinels were still on duty, even in the harsh winter weather.

They had supporters who'd help them with hot drinks and bricks to stand on, but there was also growing public anger and violence toward them. America was at war, and their protest was considered unpatriotic.

Some of the women were assaulted by members of the public and then unjustly arrested, enduring abuse in jail.

The Sentinels were tired of President Wilson not supporting their fight for a new amendment to the Constitution.

This very visible protest ensured he saw their message every time he came and went from the building.

At first, Wilson found the women's actions amusing. However, after the United States entered World War I in April 1917, the Sentinels used his own rousing war statements on their banners, embarrassing the president.

The women were courageous and determined.

Because of this, the government and the public did not forget the cause for women's suffrage during the difficult wartime years.

Fighting for the VOTE in Wartime

Many American men were called up to fight in World War One.

The NWP were angry that the President was sending their loved ones to fight for democracy in Europe while not giving the women of America **their democratic right to vote.**

While the Silent Sentinels were protesting at the White House, the two million members of the **National American Woman Suffrage Association** (NAWSA) chose less aggressive methods. They publicly supported President Wilson, even sitting down for meetings with him in the Oval Office.

NAWSA took up **war work**, like driving trucks and raising money to support American troops.

These women hoped to demonstrate **patriotism** and show that women deserved the vote because they'd taken on jobs that normally belonged to men.

MARIE LOUISE BOTTINEAU BALDWIN

Speaking the Truth of Indigenous Women's Suffrage

On August 3, 1914, when readers of the *Washington Times* turned to page nine of their newspaper, they were greeted by three photographs of the same woman.

She was lawyer Marie Louise Bottineau Baldwin, of both the Turtle Mountain Ojibwe (Chippewa) Nation and French heritage. And above the photos was a headline that would surprise many: "Indian Women the First Suffragists"

In the first photograph, Marie was dressed in a fashionable outfit of the time.

In the second, she was wearing the cap and gown of a student who had just graduated law school—the achievement that had drawn the attention of paper.

And in the third, taken when she was younger, she was wearing the traditional clothing and braided hairstyle of the Ojibwe.

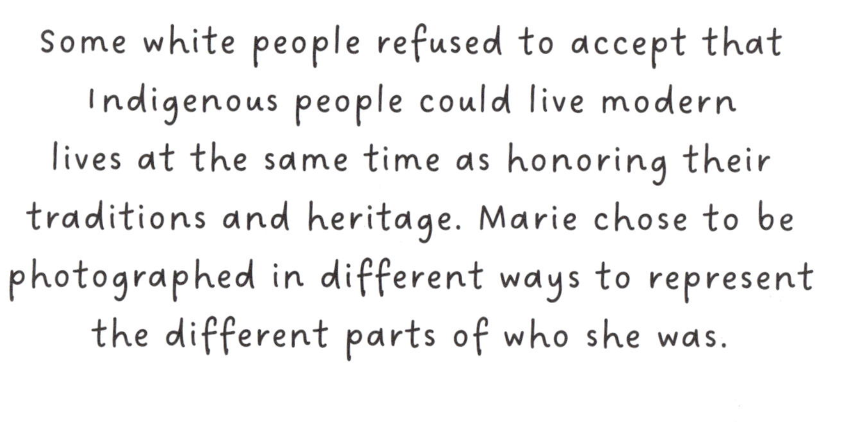

Some white people refused to accept that Indigenous people could live modern lives at the same time as honoring their traditions and heritage. Marie chose to be photographed in different ways to represent the different parts of who she was.

And she also had a clear
message: voting rights were
nothing new for Native women.

In 1914, because the press took an interest in her qualifying as a lawyer (a rare achievement for women at the time), dedicated suffragist Marie spoke out about her ancestors.

The ancestors had enjoyed power and a political voice for many centuries.

Women nominated the men who would run to be leaders. And they could also vote to have a leader removed.

Indigenous people had embraced women's suffrage a thousand years before 1914, when it was still a radical idea for some. Marie wanted to make sure the public knew.

It was not well known that the Indigenous woman had a hand in her nation's government, Marie told the *Washington Times*, **"but she did, and it was a strong one."**

The 19TH AMENDMENT
But Not the End of the Fight

The 19th Amendment said: "The right of citizens of the United States to vote shall not be denied or abridged by the United States or by any State on account of sex."

On August 18, 1920, **Tennessee** voted in favor of the new amendment to the United States Constitution.

They were the last of the 36 states the government needed to be able to make the amendment a national law.

In celebration, **Alice Paul** sewed her **36th star** onto the banner she'd been stitching as each state voted yes to the amendment.

It was a huge, hard-won victory, but it wasn't all good news. Some women still couldn't vote after this date because individual states were allowed to put other **barriers** in place to stop them.

Indigenous women weren't considered citizens of the United States, and you had to be a **citizen** to vote.

Black women, particularly in southern states, faced **literacy tests** they often couldn't pass and **taxes** they often couldn't afford.

After 1920, the fight for the vote for **ALL** women continued. But this time, it was without the support of many of the white suffragists who had already won their vote.

THE JOURNEY TO THE VOTE FOR WOMEN IN THE UNITED STATES AND THE UNITED KINGDOM

Mary Smith of Yorkshire, England, becomes the **first woman from the United Kingdom** to officially ask for the right to vote. She's refused and ridiculed by the House of Commons.

1848

Elizabeth Cady Stanton and Lucretia Mott organize the Seneca Falls Convention in New York. It's the **first local women's rights convention** to be held in the United States.

1913

Alice Paul organizes the **National Parade** in Washington, D.C. for Women's Suffrage.

1917

The Silent Sentinels begin their **peaceful protest** outside the White House.

1918 January

President Wilson gives his **support to the 19th Amendment.**

1918 February

The United Kingdom Parliament passes the **Representation of the People Act.** Women over 30 who owned property (or whose husbands did) were given the vote.

1920

The 19th Amendment becomes **part of the US Constitution.** All white women age 21 and over can vote.

1928

The **Equal Franchise Act** gives all women age 21 and over the right to vote in the United Kingdom.

1965

The **Voting Rights Act** passes in the US, protecting Black and Indigenous women and men, and women and men of color from unjust barriers to voting.

1850

The **first national Women's Rights Convention** in the United States is held in Worcester, Massachusetts. Lucy Stone is one of the organizers.

1851

Sojourner Truth delivers her **legendary speech** on women's rights in Akron, Ohio.

1868

The **first public meeting in the United Kingdom** about women's suffrage is held in Manchester, England.

1872

Susan B. Anthony is **arrested for casting a vote** in the presidential election.

1896

Ida B. Wells and others establish the **National Association of Colored Women** (later renamed The National Association of Colored Women's Clubs).

1903

Suffragette Emmeline Pankhurst forms the **Women's Social and Political Union** in the United Kingdom.

1990

The **Americans with Disabilities Act** gives voting protections to women and men with disabilities.

2013

A **United States Supreme Court ruling** weakened some protections in the Voting Rights Act, allowing states more freedom in changing voting laws. Some people argue this has once again opened the door to potential barriers that could make it harder for some groups to vote.

The struggle for women's suffrage was a global movement, waged in parliaments, streets, and homes across continents. To learn more explore beyond these stories and uncover the many women, known and unsung, who helped secure this fundamental right around the world.